A Blue House to Sleep In

Poems from Motherhood

poems by

Abby Templeton Greene

Finishing Line Press
Georgetown, Kentucky

A Blue House to Sleep In

Poems from Motherhood

Copyright © 2022 by Abby Templeton Greene
ISBN 979-8-88838-015-4 First Edition
All rights reserved under International and Pan-American Copyright Conventions. No part of this book may be reproduced in any manner whatsoever without written permission from the publisher, except in the case of brief quotations embodied in critical articles and reviews.

ACKNOWLEDGMENTS

Thank you to the following journals for publishing earlier versions of the poems listed below:

The Bangalore Review "Dreaming in Blue"

Blue Collar Review "Being Girl", previously published as "A Haunting"

Pilgrimage "Shifting"

The Elixir "Seltzer", "Above Water"

The Thought Erotic, "Cleavage"

Mom Egg Review "Crying it Out", "To Mother Like That"

The Splinter Generation "Ritual of Salt"

Wingless Dreamer "RIP Wellington Chubbs"

Publisher: Leah Huete de Maines
Editor: Christen Kincaid
Cover Art: Katie Gonzalez
Author Photo: Joseph Isaacs
Cover Design: Elizabeth Maines McCleavy

Order online: www.finishinglinepress.com
also available on amazon.com

Author inquiries and mail orders:
Finishing Line Press
P. O. Box 1626
Georgetown, Kentucky 40324
U. S. A.

Table of Contents

The Waters:

Dreaming in Blue 1

Being Girl 4

Shifting 6

Seltzer 7

Cleavage 9

Big and Small 12

Broken Wrist at Four Months 15

Naptime 17

Crying it Out 18

To Mother Like That 20

To the 15 year old Refugee Who Arrived Alone 21

My Son is Teaching Me New Words 22

Reflection 24

R.I.P Wellington Chubbs 25

God's Work 26

A Poem Called 'Almost' 27

Drowning:

Above Water 33

Like So Many Mothers 34

Over Coffee 35

YouTube Interviews 37

Emergency Training 40

A Memorial Service Love Song 41

Luck Spilling Out Like Stars 42

In Blood 43

Somewhere That is Not Here Lourdes' Daughter
    Blesses the Milk 45

Mottled Premonitions 48

Just Above the Surface:

Ritual of Salt 51

Firsts 52

On Missing Ants 54

I Cannot Die Because of the Movie *Toast* 55

Learning to Swim 56

Wedding Day Collage 59

Name Yourself 61

Meat 62

This is Why She Cannot Sleep 63

Why Painting the House Makes Me Think of Breastfeeding 64

For Risa and Desi

You must have grown out of a thousand years dreaming.

—Joy Harjo

For my Mom and Dad

Como la flor con tanto amor, me diste tú.

—Selena

Part 1: The Waters

Love is a river, flowing where we know not.
The wound is deep, yet the river is wide.

—The Wonder Years

Dreaming in Blue

The week before he was born
I dreamt only in blue,
like paint names the images collected
at the foot of my brain

:

Water's Edge, Cloudless Sky,
        Swimming Pool Blue,
Veranda Blue-Blue.
                              Water travels faster than the body,

propelling it forward—a protest.

Always different, the kinds of blue

:

water crashing through our living room window,
                      barefoot in an alley in the rain,
                            a child's body face down in a swimming pool.

Always different, the kinds of blue
not unlike the shade he was born with,
the shark blue when he came out.

                        A nurse announcing:

    your baby's life is in danger,

you need to push
now
.

                            Death rides alongside the body, a fortune

cookie decision.

Is he alive? I asked
      . . . *yeh,* my husband says

because if he said it, it would be true.
                                     When he lies, he looks left. The whites of
                                     his eyes,

the blue.

But I wasn't in the room.
I was on the lake—
goddamn Lady of Shalott,
the boat filling with blood,
their voices

falling off a dock

:

                    is he breathing?
                    I am breathing for him,
                              the tiny balloon filling his body with air
                                  pumping it in and out,
                            pumping up and down, up and

                          . . .

Did you ever dream you were drunk driving,
        and wake up in a car?

                    Did you ever dream you were drunk driving
                            and not wake up at all?

When a doctor lies, it is a diagnosis.
When a husband lies at bedside, it is a promise,   a protest,
a dream somehow
            waking,
                  from the
     blue.

Being Girl

The paper cuts on my hands
spell the word "If."

When the old woman watches
TV I turn it off to see if she'll notice.

In the living room is a stuffed chicken.

One of the brothers caught it,
wrung its neck with a bungee cord.

I once burnt the last two pieces of bread
just to see what she would do.

"¡Madre Mia!" she exclaimed,
Her forehead crawling up to the ceiling.

She shines his shoes,
tucks the boy's hair behind pink ears.

The red sores on her knuckles
are holy crosses reminding God
she is still on his side.

In this house unemployment is a disease
and a collection of plastic painted blue birds fail to find flight.

In China I am a basket
filled with rocks.
I apologize and pluck my hairs
to build the broom.

When the caseworker visits we smile,
spoons clatter against ceramic mugs.

I am the sound of wings scraping glass.
I am a beaker, waiting open mouthed.

The old woman is a Tupperware set,
all the lids sealed on too tight.

I once kissed a boy I didn't like
because he was cross-eyed
and no one else would.

Afterwards, I could feel
the shame on my cheeks,
like soap caked up on a tub wall.

That face, that face of fingernail and grit,
she makes it when she looks at me,

like even the good food
has turned bad.

Shifting

My Auntie Petra was a shapeshifter.
She used to stay at our place
in Leadville because she said
she had better luck shifting at high altitude.
My mother said she just liked the way
a mattress felt at 10,000 feet.
Auntie Petra used to watch *The Price*
is Right and yell at the screen "That ol' Bob Barker
sure is one crafty son of a bitch!"
I never heard her voice through
a telephone receiver,
she just showed up with a briefcase
and six string. "Well, I'll be! Not a penny too soon
or an uncle too late!" She used to say
when she would find some whiskey left in a flask.
Plugging her nose, she said she could tell the future,
"Smells like your mama can't cook." Petra made
her money pulling quarters from behind my ears.
"When you're older I'll give you your share, Lilly Bell."
She always left before the white hares of summer
started showing up. My mother
said it was just the way she was, but I knew
she was one of them.

It wasn't until the blizzard of '82,
coming home from school I found the jar of quarters
on our doorstep with a note that read "I'm it."
That night at dinner a saltshaker fell on its side.
Rolling around the wooden table the salt looked like snow flurries trying to escape.
That was the night our dinner table became sky
and Auntie Petra a snowstorm.

Seltzer

The surge of seltzer water
bubbling towards
the rim of my glass
reminds me of rice juice
escaping the lid of a pan. Leave it
to my mother to ruin Uncle Ben's.

She was one of those exercise freaks.
Instead of using a timer, my mother
would do sets of squats or push ups
while cooking. *A 20 minutes fish bake—*
that is definitely enough time
for a workout, she would say,
doing lunges across the linoleum kitchen floor
or dancing ferociously to one of her favorite
Latin radio stations.

Now I am mother.
And I wonder how she ever had time
for any of it. Not the treadmill
or her Jane Fonda workout tapes,
but the everyday. The time to dig
out dirt from under your fingernails,
time to quote Bashi poems,
to notice a song about bird,
to notice birds.

Seltzer water is the closest thing
to drinking electricity.
With the weather and the baby,
it tastes good just to feel this rush,
like holding a battery to my tongue
or swallowing an orchestra of bells.

I put all the glasses back
in the cupboard, each one
with its mouth locked to the shelf.

I'm tired, tired like it hurts
to blink, like each sentence
is a small boulder
rolling up my chest.

Cleavage

I thought
it was something
you bought.
Like a toothbrush,
or a new pair of socks.

Having heard my mother say it
and knowing it was good,
I announced to my 3rd grade class:
My sister has cleavage.

I didn't know what it meant
but I knew it was something to be proud of,
like setting a new double-dutch record
or holding your breath underwater
the whole lap of the pool.

*   *   *

At camp we were responsible
for splitting our own firewood.
Just swing, we were instructed,
*and let the weight of the ax drop
through your hands.*
The wood splintered and cracked
as if it had the division planned all along.

My friend and I got the bottom bunk,
the girls above us wore training bras and lip-gloss.
At night they held their hands over their mouths
not to laugh while they sprinkled salt on us
and watched as we batted at air.

The counselor told us to eat our veggies,
Carrot will make your boobs grow, she said.

The girls on the top bunk ate

whole plates of the stuff.
Instead of salt shakers,
they started smuggling
carrots out of the cafeteria:
pockets and day packs full.

*   *   *

I remember the scene in 'Mr. Mom'
when Michael Keaton looks over
his neighbor's shoulder while playing poker,
only he's not really looking
at her cards. *Are these any good?*
she asks him, *You got two pair,
you got plenty.* He answers.

*   *   *

It was in 7th grade when
Troy Thomas told me
I had nice legs.
Nice at what? I asked.
Just nice.
It was as if he had told me
I had a nice elbow
or a really great pair of knuckles.

*   *   *

I want to go back
to those middle school hallways,
to the closed doors of high school,
to that kid, before she was
girl or teen, before
she knew the presence of eyes
following her across intersections.
I want to tell her

you are more than a vessel of want,
more than a glossy photograph,
or a golden collection of cells.

I want to tell her: you are dandelion, tethered to earth
and yet you fly, like the wind that escaped.
Like the tip of sunlight balancing between dawn and day,
something no man's hand can ever touch.

Big and Small

for R

Small:
the flesh of your arm,
a boomerang stretched
across your forehead.

Small:
fists
that open and close,
that tug at the air that shapes you.

Big:
the air that shapes you,
the gasses that yield
to your existence.

Small:
your toes in your mouth,
your hands in my mouth.
I swallow your hands and birth you again.

Big:
birth,
a moaning in the night,
a hospital hallway,
a twisting inside.

Small:
your chin resting on my chest,
your belly and butt scooped up in my palm,
your pudgy feet fluttering in protest.

Small:
cell and hair follicle,
eyelid and cuticle bed,
the map of rivers inside you,
perfectly placed.

Big:
the rivers that could swallow you,
could take you to a place where you were a dream,
to a time when everyone begged
to know your name,
gender, height and weight.

Small:
height
and small weight
and small the snaps on your back,
the buckles on shoes that never touch the ground,
the dirt you collect in your tiny pockets,
the rolls of skin that pad and don't break you.

Big:
the dream where I break you,
the one where you fall off the bed
and I awake in a panic grasping
for the small parts of you.

Small:
the parts,
the belt loop,
the buttons,
the tooth of a comb,
the crumb of bread so small
only you could spot it, there
on the dining room floor,
and with your hummingbird hands
you tweezer it—
between forefinger and thumb
and pronounce it valuable,
this crumb divided 100 times,
this grain of wheat and harvest,
this molecule of sunlight
and baker's early morning.

You grasp it, keep it for hours
in the warm heart of your palm,
this crumb that is only meant for sweeping,
this crumb that is a small fraction of itself,
you study it, cradle it,
knowing it is worthy,
knowing it is bone.

Broken Wrist at Four Months

When you are four months old
I break my wrist in an indoor soccer game,
collapse on it, still clumsy
trying on my postpartum body.
The only bone I ever broke.

When you are four months old
I struggle to pry you from your car seat,
no longer able to puzzle together
the buckles that cross your chest,
to push the red buttons in and pull the handle down,
unable to lift you from the deep sink of your crib
in the night.

When you are four months old
my left hand stumbles,
attempting the responsibilities
it was never allowed: driving on its own,
striking a match,
inserting and turning the key just so.

When you are four months old
I want to pull you back
to a space where each thread of your bone
wove into mine,
to a time when tiny fists were caught
punching from the inside out,
when each eyelash was a prayer,
each cell was a pebble I threw over a bridge.

Relatives arrive unannounced,
hold you too long, and ask too many questions.
I lock us in your new room,
wishing I could scoop you back up
inside of me. Wanting to scream from a sharp tower:
She is mine! All mine!
But none of it is.

When you are four months old
a refugee girl arrives alone by raft.
She is daughter.
She too was once fabric, woven into a mother.
I want to pull her back in too,
wipe her face, cradle her.
The book of mothers is wide,
wider than a raft, wider than a sea.

When you are four months old,
I am 31. Together we are learning
to live within ourselves,
to live amongst this world of bramble,
of nylon turf and bone,
learning to point to the shiny metallic object,
to that spec of land on the horizon
and try to grasp.

Naptime

1.
Most days are spent
unloading: dishes, clothes, car seat, lunchbox Tupperware lids.
Sorting: rubber bathroom ducks, wooden blocks, napkins from dishcloths,
white gym socks with yellow lines on the toes,
white gym socks without yellow lines on the toes.

2.
Sometimes it is time of my own:
nap with the curtains pulled tight to the outside world,
an email I meant to send, a hurried shower, or call to the cable company,
a chance to shovel the walk.

3.
Today it is sunlight
streaming through our
bedroom window, green walls turned to gold.
Today it is your copper skin against mine with thick blankets piled on top,
even though today—our bodies curled up like yarn—we don't need no blankets,
this house so quiet I forget we have a kid, forget there is anything outside of this
    room,
like the mornings ten years ago in your grandmother's upstairs room, the rattling
of bed posts she never heard. I forget
like when every hour of every day was a naptime,
the whole house a cradle, and each minute was a still life hanging
from a museum wall: you crunching the apple, the taste of wine fresh on my lips.

Crying It Out

> *While it may involve some tears, sleep training isn't harmful for babies, who often learn to be super sleepers in just a few nights.*
> —www.whattoexpect.com

It is the night we read about,
the night all the moms talk about,
an episode I saw on *Super Nanny,*
and thought *What's the big deal?*

The big deal is it is 4:00 in the morning
and she's been crying since 2:00.
The big deal is with every yowl my boobs ache,
and my heart slaps me in the chest, questioning:
What have I done? What have I done? What are we doing?

`She will learn`, the doctor says—
her hands gripping the edge of her crib.
`Sleep training`, they call it—
her small body howling at the monitor,
rocking itself back and forth.

4:23 am: arms flail in desperation,
she reaches to standing,
exhausted, falls back to sitting.

4:50 am: she is up again,
having dragged herself
to the corner of the crib,
cheeks wet with fury,
her plump fingers search in the dark,
hoping for some sign of comfort,
some sign of us.

Every cell in my body wants to pull her
from the pit where dreams don't go,
pull her and wrap her in quilts
that smell like mother, but instead
I stay at my post.

I turn the fan up to high, check the clock,
try not to peak at the screen that shows me
what I don't want to see.
I curl my arms and feet around my husband
searching desperately
for someone
to mother.

To Mother Like That

I longed to be young Maria Sanchez, played by Jennifer Lopez in the 1995 movie *Mi Familia*. I longed to be that kind of mother who wrapped her son in her rebozo and cradled him all the way from Michoacán, Mexico back home to Nuestra Señora de la Reina de Los Ángeles (LA). On foot, horseback, whatever it took to survive for the pulsing beat of family. I wanted that thickness of story, to mother like a puma hunting in the night, like a vine weed creeping, steady and unnerved. I wanted to be the hero like that, to save my son from the drowning mouth of a river god, and harbor my children from the owls of borrowed time who perch ready to swoop and swallow them whole, heads-first. I wanted to mother like a shield and find my children uncaught between dirt and riverbed, released from the idea of borders and foreign land. I wanted to be the one to free them from the dark tin of a hungry morning, and let a little sunlight touch their chins. A mother like Maria Sanchez, now that would be something to be proud of—waiting with the light on, behind my apron a switchblade to survive.

To a 15 Year Old Refugee Girl Who Arrived Alone

No one leaves home unless home is the mouth of a shark.
—Warsan Shire

We want to add to you.
Want to give you a new name
and a blue house to sleep in.
We want you
                a family,
                a tree,
an arrow pointing any way
but down.
We want you:
a happy ending sentence,
a bowl of soup, a kettle without so much
screeching.
We think we hear you:
a silence, your words cut off at the tongue.
I imagine the boots caught in your gut,
imagine the barrel in your throat,
      your homeland
cupping shut the dreams of your mouth.
              I imagine the shark hunting in the night,
              your plane taking off and you're not
saying
                      again. Not saying
the last time you saw your mother's eyes,
not saying your father's dress shirt covered in sweat,
not saying yes
or no. You instead
      focus
on the sensation of flight, the growling belly that consumes you,
      the hollow force of air
just
beneath your feet.
Your feet:
just the two of them,
now:
the whole of you.

My Son is Teaching Me New Words

Apoxia,
Hypoxia,
ApGuard

On his hospital record
is the word trauma:
Traumatic birth,
stamped next to his name
the first time I saw it typed.

(Don't tell them his name).

    If you name your son before he is born
    they will steal his name away.
    If you name your son and he dies,
    the name dies with him.

Apoxia
Hypoxia
ApGuard
Cord Evulsion

I kept learning the terms
I didn't want to know.
All of the terms
and the future they could bring
followed me around
like the fear of giving birth in a car,

meanwhile
I was still in that car:
my husband still John Fucking Travolta
in *Look Who's Talking,*
not the birth we had planned on.

    If you write a birth plan,
    don't bring it to the hospital.
    No one will read it. If you dream a birth plan,
    don't write it down, don't jinx yourself.

> If you are a John Travolta fan,
> do not google 'Travolta La Quinta Inn Palm Springs'.
> Sometimes it is better not to know.
> If your son is born with a birth defect, don't google it.
> Don't google:

Apoxia
Hypoxia
ApGuard
Cord Evulsion
Multiple Sclerosis

> (Don't tell them his name,
> keep him close, like a stick to a fire,
> like a pit buried deep in the center.
> Hide him in the folds of your skin).

In Greece they name their children seven days after birth—
don't write it down, don't jinx yourself.

In Dominican Republic when a child loses a tooth,
they throw it on the roof and make a wish.

A wish like "Bring me a piece of chocolate or a golden coin,"
a wish like "Please, don't let the doctors take my son."

My son is teaching me new words:

Apoxia
Hypoxia
ApGuard
Cord Evulsion
Multiple Sclerosis
Sudden Infant Death Syndrome

so many ways to say
/'wolf'.

Reflection

The front hall mirror
is speckled with lip prints,

smudged with cream cheese
fingers.

Arms are not big enough
to reach through the mirror,

to love the whole world
the way she does.

Love—this thick jagged thing
we have learned to hold like a hot potato,

love—to her, is just
                      love, an algae slowly spreading.

RIP Wellington Chubbs

Death remains. It comes on sudden and leaves the house still, so quiet. Even if you try to pretend that there is a cat in the yard, chasing crickets, it's too still, too quiet. And the skinny wicker chair, the space he used to fill, is a gaping hole, like the one your husband dug, late at night with a pick ax borrowed from the neighbor, the headlights from the car shining off it. We were grave robbers on a school night, like we were watching someone else's life through a binocular lens. Like the hole she referenced, her hummingbird body, not yet three, just a bit bigger than his, when she demanded a shovel to dig him up because she didn't want him stuck living in a hole. An almost three year old, rocking and crying in the night *I want my cat, I want my cat,* wanting her cat. You don't think of these things, not until after you have gone through it, you don't image having to explain to her why her cat doesn't snuggle her at night, or run to her when she calls his name at the backdoor, you don't think about how you will chose to explain death; this glacier that keeps melting, this boat that keeps arriving.

Because it seems the right thing to do, you break her from her sleep to show her the stiff limbs, and sinking tail, the tire track squished innards. Because it is better she sees it with her own eyes, better she waves goodbye in the midnight of the backyard, before surrendering to her bed. It is the farmer in you, the survivor, the part of you that wishes you had some greater context of God, of life, it is that part of you that wakes her in the night to show her the gritty teeth of life. To do this harsh and cruel and beautiful teaching, crossing your fingers as you tell her, that maybe it really will be all right.

God's Work

> *Are you ready to wake up for your life and not just to your life?*
> —Kat Lee

It is early morning, it is still outside before
the cars list up at the stop sign,
cartoons are loud,
the counter sticky.
She wants to do the cleaning,
wants to do the tidying up.

Thinks: put dirty dishes in sink away.
Thinks: put clean dishes on drying rack away.
Thinks: pick blueberries off the vine and squish them in between toes,
cork it, ferment it, guzzle it till you stain your teeth, put things back where they don't go,
better yet don't put things back at all,
open the front door and sing.
Sing loud, louder. Dance
                                       like a montage, like a protest
like a fist in the air, like a pandemic, like a rally: run.
Run like pavement, like a quarantine, like a live newscast: run.

*

Outside in the garden
the dirt doesn't pile up the same.
Outside the infestation of ants
are just
                         ants.

It is still early morning
and she is still stuck in the decision of how to live her life:
this morning and
all the ones to come.

A raven crows,
a squirrel runs on a wire with the shell of a grapefruit in its mouth.
Her son points and calls it
'fox'.

A Poem Called 'Almost'

for Desi, for Jules

I wrote this poem after giving birth.
Like right after birth,
like thirsty in the delivery bed with blood crusted to my feet-after-birth.
I remember wishing someone would wet a wash cloth and scrub my feet clean.
The nurse asked if I wanted anything
and I asked for water.
We can't give you water, she told me.
Just like they couldn't hold my hand
because they were scrubbed up.
So I asked for a pen and paper
and I wrote this poem.
Only it wasn't this poem
because in this poem I am explaining
the writing of this poem,
But in the real poem

```
I wrote:
It was his birthday,
the day we almost lost our son.
The day my husband drove like a Hollywood movie:
me, the Jennifer Anniston character, ( only rounder,
much rounder in the face)sitting shotgun, clutching my
belly and crotch,
yelling for directions from police officers,
an emergency room entrance,
almost a minivan birth.

Almost—with your talons clutching,
your tight grip of an umbilical cord wrapped two times
round his unassuming neck.
Almost—the cord breaking, stretched too thin by time.
Almost—his skin as white as hospital sheets,
but it wasn't white,
my husband will tell me: blue,
not unlike the blue of my dreams
```

the one where our house floods with rainwater.
But he wouldn't call it rain either,
rather a flood,
a massive dismission of blood.

Almost—a 10 lbs baby, 9 lbs and 8 ounces
the nurse telling me: *your baby's life is in danger—you
need to push now.*

So you do.
You push. You push like the lions are at your back,
like the hounds are inside you, like the hooves are in
your stomach: all claw and gnarl and bits of hair locked
in your teeth. You push like that.
Trying to beat the almosts.

I called the poem "Almost", and used the word repeating.
Only I didn't write it out full, because I was too
exhausted, I wrote it out "A-mst". Like skipping "l and "o"
would save so much energy, would save so much blood.
It didn't work.
When you take out "l" and "o"
you still pass out on the hospital floor,
you still need a blood transfusion.
Later I wondered whose blood it was
and did she or he almost.
Later in the poem I tried to wrap things up,
explain some of the happenings to the reader:

And then
it is done.
You know he is here
because they have stopped prying you.
This little you that they pump air into
his dad's nose, his sister's face.

The fear of the almosts sits

```
like a windowsill,
like the forcep scar on his skull, reminding.
```

Later I read the poem at the gallery,
Dona Laurita's daughter came up to me.
She loved the poems, she said.
She was a musician, 16, beautiful with curly musician hair.

A year and a half later she died of brain cancer.
Her mother closed the gallery.
Before, I had written:

```
So you wait
somehow negotiating the space around your house
waiting for each minute to pass
so you will be further from it,
the 'it' of the almost.
Sitting in the now—in the finality of life.
In the fucking blessing that is,
and not what almost wasn't.
```

In the poem called 'Almost', no one dies.
But that was just a poem.

Part 2: Drowning

Everywhere was a shallow sea.

—Kali Fajardo-Anstine

Above Water

It's hard being in love
with sand. I always have to
be the one to turn off the lights.
It is hard to say: I love
you equally, for richer,
or for poorer, wet as well
as dry. At couples therapy
you get in my eye, steal
the bed sheets in your sleep.
"Did it ever occur to you,"
the therapist says, "that love
might not conquer all?" stumbling
around in the dark I find you've
given yourself away again:
a child's sandbox, an hourglass,
the Pacific Coast. You are absent
but coarse grains stay
stuck in my teeth.

Like So Many Mothers

To Larcenia Floyd, aka Miss Cissy Jones Floyd

Thank God George Floyd's mother wasn't alive to watch when they hunted and preyed on him, when they wrung the last drops of air out of him like a dirty rag, and dug their hands like teeth through his warm chest to extract the whole of his fleshy heart for all the world to see. Thank God.

Thank God she didn't collapse from the phone call, buckle at the knees onto kitchen floor. Thank God she didn't stutter to take back time, to dig the vision of him up out of the dirt with her bare fingernails. Thank God.

I want to thank God she didn't wake in the night—like so many mothers—her dreams an ambulance to a time when she could armor him, when she could pull tight the small hand that fit inside her palm like a seed, like the curl of a leaf, to a time when she could still check his chest in the night, to be sure it would gently rise and fall, gently rise and fall again, thank God.

But we know she was there. She saw it all like any coyote hunting or redwood root—she was there pushing and pumping the air back into him, pushing and pumping; hoping for the rise and the fall.

Again and again and again they killed him in front of us.
Again and again and again she would have saved her son.

I want to tell her something, this mother I will never know, I want to tell her: enough. Enough of the sky and its stars. Enough with this earth that is an unworthy witness to sorrow. Enough of the howling we have caused; tonight is a good night for fire, to throw something that will burn.

Over Coffee

> *I don't know what I should talk about—about death or about love? Or are they the same? Which one should I talk about?*
> —Svetlana Alexievich from *Voices from Chernobyl*

I had coffee with your mom today—
holding my breath for your return.

She swears it wasn't you; wasn't you who fell out that window.
She says your wife shaved her head, buried her hair along with your ashes.

The rest of you she keeps in a vial inside her medicine cabinet,
leaving something behind, something that can't be shattered.

I want to write you into existence,
but that is not how time works.

400 people walked through the theater remembering you.
Waited to witness the face that used to be you, the body no longer occupied.

I want to write these words in the present tense, but that is not the way
the English language works.

"Save travels" your mom texted, though it was supposed to read "safe."
Save travels, like save your last breath,

save your sons face squished up next to yours,
save him from jumping out a window, save him from the impact,

from the inner bleeding, unseen. Behind the mirror, a small film canister of you.
Now you are little bits of bone and teeth.

You used to be skin and movement. You used to sound.
400 people, like a parade, a dragon. Years earlier you told her

*I love music because you used to sing me to sleep,
even though you couldn't carry a tune.*

These words are written in the past, because it's a quote,
because the quotation marks the beginning

and the end. The end.
She shakes her head, thinking

maybe it was time to pull tight the drawstring of your mind,
the lamp of your body left on too long.

Behind the mirror, the light gets through, behind the profile of head and shoulders
400 people march, rotate to witness.

Her hair *used to be* long. Now she is bald. Now her hair grows
underground, tucked inside a metal box.

We use 'used to' to talk about things that happened in the past—
actions or states—that no longer happen now.

Like you. You no longer happen now. So, we (present tense) dig a hole,
we (present tense) plant a tree. We (present tense) sing happy birthday

to your son.

YouTube Interviews

i.
Интервьюер: Откуда вы делаете свое внимание, свою мотивацию, свою музу?

Interviewer: From where do you draw your focus? Your motivation, your muse?

Kaz: Свет тела не может сопротивляться, мы можем сопротивляться только себе на этом временном уровне так долго, какое-то время. То же и с искусством, с искусством я - пешка вселенной, перестройка сердца. Великие кончики пальцев Бога гладят меня, эфемерные и всеобъемлющие. Когда я спрашиваю, здесь ли он, ответа нет, но когда в комнате тихо, музыка все равно остается.

Caz: The light of the body cannot resist, we can only resist ourselves on this temporal level for so long, for some time. It is the same with art, with art I am the pawn of the universe, a perestroika[1] of the heart. God's great fingertips stroking through me, ephemeral and all encompassing. When I ask if he is here, there is no response, but when the room is quiet, music still remains.

Интервьюер: Как вы узнали историю о Черном и Симпсоне?

Interviewer: How did you learn of the story of Black and Simpson?

Kaz:
Где мы узнаем о чем-нибудь в эти дни, когда все великие гобелены уже были сплетены? Я мог сказать, интернет, или я не мог. Я мог бы сказать, что отец отца отца моего отца сказал мне, но это оставило бы матери.

Caz: Where do we learn of anything these days when all the great tapestries have already been woven? I could say the internet or I could not. I could say my father's father's father's father's father, but that would leave out the mothers.

интервьюер: что еще? Расскажите нам о человеке за занавеской.

---

[1]Perestroika: *noun*
   1.   (in the former Soviet Union) the policy or practice of restructuring or reforming the economic and political system.

Interviewer: What else? Tell us about the man behind the curtain.

Kaz: Я люблю свою жену и сына. Мы помещаем в квартиру рождественскую елку, мой сын преследует белок вокруг парка, в его улыбке он - его мать, в его глазах вы все еще можете видеть меня.

Caz: I love my wife and son. We are putting up a Christmas tree in the apartment. My son chases squirrels around the park, in his smile he is his mother, in his eyes you can see me.

ii.
Watching the interviews of you,
in Moscow, speaking in Russian,
you feel further away than I remember,
like maybe you did
jump
five
       stories

down,
       or up

                                          or out

Like
Mayb
e there
was mo

re to the vi
nes of your
life than an y o
f us could have
ever seen: lovely
and brilli ant and
 ch ok   ing
   and cho
   king,
       and
    cho   k
         i   n   g
        as
         they
      grew.

Emergency Training

for Caz

It was an emergency simulation training put on by FEMA at George Washington High School—a chance for students to get certified on a Saturday, a good thing to put on their resume. I was walking through, trying to find the Language Learner Training Course I was required to take and it all seemed fine until I saw an arm on the cafeteria floor, lying at a 90 degree angle, a lunchroom table on its side, blocking the rest of the body.

And it made me think of your arm, Caz, your hand in mid-air grasping. For what: Your son? Your wife? The tail end of a comet? It made me think of you wanting to take it back. Wanting to clutter the countertop, to close the window, head back to bed. What did you believe? That you were a large cat jumping from a perch, believe your body was smoke billowing, thinning and becoming air? Did you believe that you—of gravity and weight—could also be opposite: something winged and weightless, a thing of flight.

I made it to my training, but I was not in the classroom. I too had turned opposite: weightless, billowing underwater, holding my breath, trying to make it to the fifteen-minute break to exhale. Trying to make it through the next thought of you, paddling and swimming and searching and holding my breath for you.

A Memorial Service Love Song

The hairs fall from my head in black clumps with more white hairs than I expected woven through. I tilt my head and rest it on your stomach while you scratch the blade back and forth across my scalp. I wish we had more than Saturday afternoons for these moments. The moment you tell me *You're cute*, like we are not seven years married with two kids napping. Like we are not on our way to our friend's memorial service, but like we just met. Like it's the first time you told me, and your eyes and the corners of your lips curl up while we curled up under your grandmother's quilts in her upstairs bedroom, in the bedroom I first learned to love you in. It was a time before we were growing used to funeral services, to dressing up just to bend down and cloak ourselves in dirt.

Later, when I see the old friends from high school, I am surprised that they too are growing in all of the ways: up, out, in. Like the cancer that we could never see, like the cancer that grew and grew and grew until it was an invasive cottonwood, until it was all roots. The coolest kid, now just looks old. The hottest girl—just tall.

It's late when we return. You don't say much, as to not wake the kids. You don't say much when you sneak into the shower, the water washing the small hairs off my neck, rinsing away the stain of a mother's perfume, trying to roll aside the heavy boulder of death. *You're cute*, you whisper, your words one moment closer to filling the distance between the stars, your words, like the rest of us, slipping down the drain

Luck Spilling Out Like Stars

I don't usually gamble,
but the day he jumped
out of the apartment window,
I bought a lotto ticket
because,
if anything can happen,
then
shit,
anything
can happen.

*

Almost a year since you died, the moon looked the same as it did when I heard the news.
Is that a thing? Does the moon look the same a year later?

On Friday I saw your name on a license plate.
That shit hasn't happened since last summer and today that song stuck in my head.

If you think it's a sign, then it is one:

Hello Cazie!
How's the weather up there?
It's windy as fuck down here
and we are missing you.

*

Always hang your horseshoes
with the 'U' facing up,
that way the luck doesn't fall out.
And I trusted her, a Lakota Sioux
should know about horses, I thought.
But after the incident
she started switching things around in the apartment.
Always leave at least one horseshoe with its feet on the ground, she told me,
No one can have good luck
all the time.

In Blood

for Destini Martinez, RIP

I was jealous when I saw her FB post:
the photo of her tattoo,
jealous of a love like that.
Even though I was her teacher,
14 years older, I was jealous, like maybe I was missing something:
'*Ezekiel* in tall thick letters
made no mistake who her man was,
who belonged to who.

Looking at her photo: so sure and confident,
I was jealous of a love like that.
My husband and I,
our love felt less than, simpler:
holding hands in bed at night, planning the weekly dinner menu.
Less star crossed then years before,
no longer a yell from the rooftops kind of love,
more comfortable than that, like family.

I didn't know then
that across the desert of her skin she had tattooed
the name of the man who would kill her,
like a fingerprint, like a police report:
the blood from the needle the same blood
that would seep from her like a bullet hole wound.

And now it seems more obvious, the postscript beneath:
We got a love like no one else, Babe. Love you, Zeke.
More surrender, than love,
more of a car alarm in the night, more shield meant to block,
meant to say: *Look, Babe! Look how much I love you!*

Don't throw me against the wall tonight,
cuz I got your name across my chest, Babe. Don't
pull my hair out at the root tonight, not when the kid is awake,
not with apartment walls

so thin.
Don't you think there's no one else, Babe,

cuz our love can't be measured in rims or gold or diamonds but in flesh and bone and blood. And blood, Babe, always in blood.

Somewhere That is Not Here Lourdes' Daughter Blesses the Milk

> *There are an estimated 58,000 admissions of pregnant women into jails and prisons every year.*
> —*The Prison Policy Initiative*

I was there
the day the baby arrived
like a phone call or a basket.

I was tutoring the boys, the new uncles:
such sweet boys with wide smiles, so behind in math.
Two hours each.
Two hours is a long time to make up multiplication games,
four hours if you multiply the two sessions by two.

A prison pregnancy, that's what they called it, nacimiento encarcelada,
the guard drove Lourdes' daughter to the hospital,
her baby swimming inside her the whole way.
Only the guard, a doctor and her
allowed in the room, 24 hours later the same officer drove her back,
12 lbs lighter, no more of that swimming inside her.

And the house?
Already so tight with humans and corners and then
this small delivery, this blessed heaviness, like a rock.
One day Lourdes was mother, the next grandmother
and mother, again. A double duty mother
now.

She let the boys skip their sessions that day
and asked me for a favor.

I drove us north on the 405 to Reliable Appliance,
where the neighbor said she could get a good deal.
I drove because I had a car and I speak both languages.

The deals were good and she had cash, only thing was
my '94 subaru wasn't big enough to hold a washing machine,
only thing was she wasn't sure the breaker could even handle it-
not with the lights on anyway and she already had a water bill
on the verge of spilling over.

We drove home empty handed, but nothing was empty:

she had a trash bag full of baby clothes, knitted caps and blankets,
she had a list of different kinds of formula, a crumpled paper with visiting hours.
She had her own heart, which she divided into pieces and placed on the kitchen
    table:
a two top in a home trying to feed 7, now 8.
A table she filled and filled again because she had magic
enough to turn an empty pantry into something,
but not enough magic to move a washing machine,
not enough magic to free a daughter from a prison cell.

She had two boys with all the wrong numbers, and all the right dreams.
She had a bathtub she had washed everyone else's hair in,
had a scrap of moon she could see from her backdoor,
and hands that smelled like hot oil.

She had this city air that she breathed each morning and the dream
that the molecules she exhaled were the same ones her daughter inhaled
when Lourdes wasn't allowed in the hospital room.
She had a collection of time, time to worry about that same birthing room
and had they shackled her daughter to the bed? Did anyone brush her hair back,
offer a sip of water, let her hold the baby?

Lourdes had a new baby now
and a collect call from a mother who was searching her cell for that smell,
that same sweet smell that filled my backseat.
Or maybe she was sitting unsupervised
in a lactation room, patiently pumping and blessing the milk,
she too imagining each breath she drew was a particle,
that was a molecule,

46

that was free,
like if she breathed deep enough she could reach the ocean,
she could even swim.

Mottled Premonitions

In an under-heated swimming pool
the Russian synchronized swim team
caught their breath.
One of them removes her cap,
thinks she sees her mother's reflection:
a stamp of navy amongst such luminescence.

During their routine rain falls
outside of Moscow, a housewife
tips a subway saxophonist one ruble,
a live-in boyfriend becomes a father.
There are rivers just under the surface.
Just under the surface, are rivers:
ammonium, nitrate, phosphorus,
flowing towards saltwater streams.

Underwater she sees her, twenty years younger:
her hands float amongst waves of chlorine,
fleeting like the mist that balances between day and night.
The impression leaves a speckled imprint
on her eyelids. *People can be like that,*
she thinks to herself, *showing up*
like a ripped out book page,
like a prayer, already drowning
before it has left her lips.

Part 3: Just Above the Surface

in the boat of myself,
no light and no land anywhere,
cloudcover thick. I try to stay
just above the surface,
yet I'm already under
and living with the ocean

—Mewlana Jalaluddin Rumi

Ritual of Salt

A former lover enters my apartment window and says
"You always did look better in blue." He starts taking
photographs of my surroundings—an obnoxious habit.
It is night and there is no one left on the block except
him and me, this former lover who is a gate that won't close.
He reminds me that raindrops always appear bigger
from below. "I should know," he says, "because I am a camera
lens in a storm lying on my back." I think he is a salt shaker
fallen on his side. Sometimes I can be found waiting for grains
to escape, other times I am dressed in a uniform, sweeping him
into a dust pan. Climbing out the window he says "Orange Rind",
that's what he used to call me or "She Who Trips on Carpet",
"Why didn't you ever plant that money tree, like I told you?
You could be rich by now, instead of just a dreaming poet."

Firsts

for Gloria

I.
It was him again,
like an old fender
scraping the street.
In the dream he says
give it back,
did she still have his
condom
and could she
give it back?
The one that remained
like a finger in a socket—
nine hours twisting
up and up inside of her.
17 and she searches:
the bed sheets,
between the mattress
and the box spring,
pulls each hair from her head,
shakes all the sand
from her summer dress
in hopes
of discovery,
no, not discovery—
rather a panicked
rage of denial.

(It is in a roadside bathroom
when she gets enough nerve
to reach into the deepest
cavern of herself
and finally put her hands
where only he had been.
She pulled it out
and into the metal trash can

on the side of the stall door
all in one fluid motion,
like she had practiced this
ceremony her whole life,
like if she did it fast enough,
it wouldn't really count.)

II.
The nurse told her not to worry,
patted her on the back.
But nurses are absent
on the way to Study Hall
when she is uncaught
vomiting in a high school trash can.

III.
Unknowing,
the morning of the miscarriage
he gave her a ride to school.

On Missing Ants

> *Governor Jared Polis orders Colorado to stay home in bid to slow Coronavirus outbreak.*
> —*Denver Post*, March 25th, 2020

When my daughter was two winged ants invaded her bedroom—
only at night, in the hot months,
they came in through the cracks, climbed the walls,
the windowsill, crossed the deserted plain of ceiling.
I only saw them when putting her to bed.
Right when I was convincing her of safety
and dreams, I would see one, then another,
next thing ten or twenty
scattering the perimeters.
A connected intelligence:
killing one, would only bring more.

Five years later,
we snuggle in the same corner of the same room.
It is still the long end of winter and I remember that I have forgotten about the ants.
Now I worry about the things I cannot see:

was she wearing a glove when she touched the guard rail?
Did she use her hands to take off her shoes?
For how many days do we leave the shoes out in the sun—
the soles facing God with their mouths sinking into earth?
Did I wash her hair, her clothes? If I can't wash the clothes,
put them in the sun. Put my body in the sun. My body is the sun.
My body is a star. Don't go outside.
Don't leave the house. You are safest at home.
We are safest at home, unless
it has already crept in:
coming in through the cracks, climbed the walls,
the windowsill, crossed the deserted plain of ceiling.
Ceiling:
our one precious sky.

I Cannot Die Because of the Movie *Toast*, A Basement Quarantine

Did you ever watch the movie *Toast?*
The story of Chef Nigel Slater,
a young boy abandoned to lovelessness
after his mother's death.

I cannot die because of *Toast*.
How could I do that?
Go and die on my kids?
Did you ever read the book Voices from Chernobyl?

This feels like that. Here we are:
afraid to hug each other, afraid to harvest and gather
the potatoes from good soil,
to touch a small segment of orange.

A perfectly good orange—poisoned from one touch.
I try to rest. They say rest, drink plenty of fluids.
They say they will call with positive test results,
send an email with negative. I check my email

like a pulse. I try to watch TV, but every scene
someone hugs someone or kisses them off to school,
or eats a taco without washing their hands.
It is hard to watch. Upstairs is a volcano:

kids laughing and jumping and tickling and stomping and crying, my kids
wrapped up in my husband's chaotic love;
anything to keep them out of the basement.
In the night there is the sound of my own coughing,

and the drawn out hum of sirens going to battle.
I want to ask, if I die, who will peel the oranges?
Who will pluck them from the supermarket bin?
Who, with her hands made of earth, will make the toast,

spread the butter just so and watch them,
with their corn kernel teeth, as they crunch in?
I want to ask a God we call Netflix, a God with a thousand eyes,
will any of us ever share a taco again?

Learning to Swim

1.
I am in the surf
  the wave coming,
    double set.
It is big,
I know it is big. Try to grab
      her
        in her mermaid bathing suit
  the wave grabs her first.
She is under.
    I think I can find her easily—
the wave will push her back,
we will collide, I think.
      Arms wide,
        ready to receive her but
    it's just water.
It is all just water.

  A four and a half year old body
    a spec in an ocean the size of an ocean.
I am
in the surf
      flailing, tornadoing for one
    tiny part to grasp: toe, elbow,
bow on the back of her suit where the straps criss cross.
Nothing.
      In the space that should be a small human is water
    murky and white and foam.
It is all water and wave and sand.
     I am spinning now: sure she
is behind,
        when I am in front
in front when
      I am behind.
It is all water and wave and sand.
I am desperate,
    grabbing at all the blue like air.

Counting now—starting the count: knowing every second
1—
2—
What if I hit 3? If I hit 3/FUCK/where is she/where is she/where is she/it is all water.
All just water/wave/and sand/until just like it started—/she bobs
/bobs up like the
        lobster cage I prayed for.
Eyes wide, mouth gaping
she surrenders like a wet scrap of cloth in my arms/
saying nothing, nothing to say,
both knowing enough for today.

2.
When we took the kids
to Nicaragua I thought of you
forever traveling the globe,
trotting through airports and borders with
your wife and son.
I thought of you and how you ended:
a shadow of yourself,
a chalk outline on a Moscow sidewalk—
thought you knew how to swim.

Your wife says it was an LSD flashback,
Yvonne, a Russian conspiracist,
claims he saw a hand print:
ottolknul; shoved.
I keep thinking of your kitchen countertop: clean, cleared for a smooth exit.
They say it couldn't have been a fall because of the trajectory.
The trajectory of it would require
a jump.
When you cliff dive off the point at Playa Gigante
you have to jump out,
                    a dive,
                                a decision,
                                          a trajectory.
Your mom doesn't want to talk about it.

When we took the kids
to Nicaragua I felt so removed:
the Contra War has nothing to do with your death,
I was guilty being there,
in a space so hot, so humid, so far from Russia.
So far from the photo that has become the memory that was before
just your face.

3.
They say that grief is love in the past tense.
Love, they call it, trying to surface.
But I say bullshit. Grief is the brick pulling us down.
Grief is the fear of carrying your body like a corpse,
the fear of your elbow disjointed on cold cement,
the fear of her face down in the water,
a fear unbearable to ferry.

She doesn't want to talk about it.
She doesn't want to say the words:
What if I am the name in the reason
the rocks were placed in your pocket?
What if I
am the rocks?

Wedding Day Collage

for Aly, our little Chickadee

The aunties drove the four hundred miles to deliver the wedding quilt.
It was hard getting here
                                               her sister in law paid for the gas.
There's been a lotta deaths lately, back home,
                                    on the reservation
but we wanted to come for Alison
                              for Aly.

~

Aly told me to talk to water.
I smiled.
No, Literally: Talk. To. Water.

Hello Water, please wash away self-doubt,
self-judgment, fear.

She told me to tell the water what to fill me with,
so it doesn't just fill with the same shit.

Hello Water, please fill me with
calm, and confidence.
Please fill me with the strength of a tank of gas,
please wrap me like a wedding quilt.

~

In the basement is a quilt with the names of everyone she ever loved stitched
along the seam. Some of the names she still loves, some have come undone.

The threads of marriage can come undone. Is it marriage we are celebrating
or the beauty of youth, the illusion of time?

~

Hello Water, please wash away

self-doubt, judgment, fear,
the fear of running out of gas,
the fear of coming undone.

The aunties with their hair braided like ribbons,
their eyes thick with story,
they made the drive anyway, because her father couldn't:
                            There's been a lotta deaths lately, back home.

Water, please help me make this memory a story,
help me make this story a song, please
fill me up with time.

Driving home, they crossed over highways.
A highway is like a bridge, but without water.
Without water
                        there is no prayer.
~

Water, pray for me.
Pray for me like you aren't water,
pray for me like you are an auntie, sewing at night on a reservation.

Pray for me like your hands are calloused and worn, and you make the quilt anyway,
pushing your thin slipper to cold metal—the hum of the machine your heart:
pulsing and remembering your brother, her father, a man who was good at running,
a man who was good at showing up sometimes.
You hum and pulse and you pray for more, Water, more for her:
more rooms to fill, more people to fill them with, more doors to shut
and locks that hold. You pray like that, like a marriage vow,
like a wish you hope sticks to a star. And you pray that all the goodness keeps,
wrapped around her like a shoulder, like a galaxy.
Pray for me like that, Water, like I am good in this world,
like all that is in this world is
holy and raw and good.

Name Yourself

I am water.
    I am animal vegetable miracle
        like the book we read
                one summer
                   and decided we would be
      farmers,
    like Barbara Kingsolver and her family.
But I can't be a farmer
because I am water.
I am water
    like drops of rain
        landing.
            Like gallons of the stuff
      drowning,
    but I can't drown
because I am water.
I am water.
    I am seeping in between
        stretching the legs of myself,
            like smoke filling the room
        but I can't be smoke
because I am water.
I am water
    like I never was before
        like I never was an ocean,
      an eyelash,
        a horizon.
                Like I never was a body made of water.
                   Like I never was a percent: 60,
          or a prayer before a meal,
        or a copious flow.
      I am water
        like a memory spilling,
      like a flood remembering,
    like a jar emptying
but I can't be empty
because I am water
I am.

Meat

From the onions cooking on the stove,
mountain sunset over a rectangular table,
Spanish language and German picture books.
She is from the grandmother—
shooting squirrels with a shotgun,
and nailing all the tails to the barn wall—
such a sweet meat.

She is from immigrants whose names are etched
on a list at Ellis Island, who worked as telephone operators.
She is from women always working,
she is from mothers always working,
is from a coffee table that floated across a river on a raft.

She is from pin cushion
from a golden peso tied tight to a wrist,
she is from a roast in a pan
and the whole weeks paycheck spent at the bar,
from a second family two towns over
and a phone call from a woman she never knew.

She is a cuckoo clock that makes no sound,
that sits in a basement unhung.

She is from a rack of antlers
they say her grandfather shot.
She is from the time spent wondering:
whose family ate the meat
and who kept the bones?

This is Why She Cannot Sleep

for my AWA women

Because somewhere a dog is barking.
Because there are emails not yet read,
because there are emails not yet written.
Because a TV is on and no one is watching,
because a TV is on and everyone is watching.

This is why she cannot sleep
because the kids are asleep
so this is her only chance
to see herself alone in the mirror,
to count her breaths in and out,
to put a record on and sing

like a 7th grade choir.
This is why she cannot sleep
because there is a child on a reservation
whose brother just hung himself.
Because there is a child down the road
who is thinking about

hanging himself.
Because she has no brother.
This is why she cannot sleep
because something got stuck
and needs a good tugging.
Because there is a rally going on

inside her heart. Because
there are too many kids in this bed,
because she is busy doing the math inside her head.
Because—if mother buries child, then I ask you
was it all for nothing? Then I ask you,
do *any* of the salmon make it?

Why Painting the House Makes Me Think of Breastfeeding

I have known this color, have longed for it from the deep pit of winter.
I have known this color like a seal swimming,

like sky hitting ocean waves.
I have longed for waves.

Denver, Colorado is not a place of ocean,
not a place of seagrass, hot sand,

not a place of tidepools.
I have longed for tidepools.

Longed for low tide, and a rainbow of jellyfish
even if they sting.

I have longed for eating a whole blueberry pie out of a tin with a best friend.
I have longed for a best friend—

her son swimming inside of her in Brooklyn, New York,
a gray swaddling blanket waiting like a shelf.

I have longed to be a shelf.
I have longed for this color like a wetsuit,

like a grown up with a suitcase.
Like a grown up with a suitcase, I remember this color before,

before we were mothers and grownups,
before the tiny pull of fists on our skin and dress fringes,

when our backdrops were just blue, like all the time in the world-blue,
and our days were tall. Tall sea grass days, swaying, they shook like seeds,

and looking only forward
we jumped straight in.

Acknowledgements:

I want to thank the many writing communities I have been so blessed to be a part of and have in my life. Aly Two Eagles, Hallie Haglund and Mara Sobesky, the original writers group. Thank you Aly, for letting me tell some of your stories, for teaching me how to live my creative life.

Sheila Mulligan and Catherine O'neale Thorn for making me a believer in the power of the word. The Florence Crittenton and Coliseum Street School Communities.

Antioch University Los Angeles where I earned my MFA. Lauren Marie Schmidt, Amy Pimentel, LaToya Jordan, Lisa Cheby, Jacqui Morton, Kate Bast, Sandra Rivera, Carol Potter, Eloise Kelin Healy, Richard Garcia and David Hernandez, and my Cobalt Blue Cohort.

Courtney Morgan, who shows me how to live as a writer, how to balance the worlds of life admin, writing and mothering. Who reminds me to look at the moon.

Lauren Marie Schmidt for teaching me to push past all of the barriers, to keep writing and submitting.

The Lighthouse Community of Writers for propelling me forward, for making me feel seen and the work real. To Dan Manazneras for asking me on stage one night "Tell us about the next book? Because I know there is going to be another book."

The Amherst Writers and Artists community for loving the work, for showing me how to live my dream day in and day out, to Maureen Buchannon Jones, Betsy Abrams, Belinda Edwards, and Robin Galguera, my roomie, and mentor.

Ellen Parman, my first draft reader, I do not know where I would be in this life without you. Thank you for promoting me and encouraging my writing, you are the treasure. Angeles Miron Figueroa for encouraging me and paving the path for women artists. Lori Patricacca for giving me so many rides and reasons to write. Little Leigh for the inspiration, for doing hard things. Unique Flores and Susan Fabian and the Ashley community for allowing me the gift of time. ABC for the encouragement.

The Haglund family for providing me with the gift of space and solitude. Polina, Katy, John and Caz, Dona Laurita and Jules. Thank you for knowing the healing of art, for letting me tell a small bit of your stories. Steph Dixon and Brady Grant, Prodigy Coffeehouse.

My mighty family: Naechi, Risa and Desi, for the stories, the time, the inspiration and the fuel. You three are the fruit on the tree. Thank you Naechi for believing in our biggest dreams, for carving out our creative lives together.

My sister, Molly Templeton Rutledge, for always telling me "That's awesome!", for teaching me about motherhood. Thank you to Molly and Tom for reminding me to dream big. Thank you, Macy, for promoting my books.

My parents, Bonner and Liz Templeton for prioritizing creativity over academics, for always honoring story telling, laughter and love. For my mom, the best mom I know.

All of my friends and family and many communities. Thank you for seeing me and my passion and for always asking about my writing. Thank you for reading my work, and coming to readings. Meghan Tappan MacDonald, JoJo, Stephanie Two Eagles, Ruthie, Diego and Tio Kee for always asking. Michael Templeton for honoring my work. Auntie Bon for showing me how to live as a writer. Thank you to my Templeton family, The Feuersingers, The Warner Carrillos, The Greenes, The Orozcos. Thank you to Finishing Line Press for creating such an important and powerful space for writers and readers. Thank you, dear reader, for reading this work.

And of course, since this is a book about motherhood, thank you to all of my mother figures, my grandmothers, my grandfathers, my great-grandmothers, my great grandfathers, all those who mothered before me. Thank you to Joy, my other mother, for mothering me as well. Thank you Risa and Desi, for making me Mother.

One night at dinner we were talking about our favorite things to do. When I asked my children what they thought my favorite thing to do was, I was appalled by their responses: "Clean, fold laundry, go to bed." This was such an eye opener for me. I realized I had been keeping hidden my most favorite thing from my kids. I thought about what values I was teaching my children and at that moment I decided to make writing a family thing. Saturday mornings I started writing and submitting. When my daughter asked what I was working on I told her gradious things like "living my best life". And, she would leave me alone (for the most part). No more (well, fewer) demands for juice or pretzels, instead they were excited by my excitement. They too became wrapped tight in the thick wedding quilts of the creative, in looking at the world and tilting their heads till they see it just right, just the way they imagine it might be.

Abby Templeton Greene is the author of three books of poetry: *A Blue House to Sleep In, Prayer from a Magdalena Jail Cell* and *An Avocado Slowly Falling*, a book of bilingual poems written in English and Spanish. Her work has been published in *McSweeneys, Calyx Journal, RATTLE, Pilgrimage, The Wazee, The Mom Egg Review* and other journals. She was the recipient of the 2012 Sixfold Writers contest prize for poetry, the 2011 Lighthouse Writers Seven Deadly Sins Writing Contest, and a finalist in the Blast Furnace Chapbook competition.

Abby lives in Denver, Colorado with her partner and two young children. She received her Bachelor's Degree from Gettysburg College in Latin American Studies and Spanish and earned an MFA from Antioch University Los Angeles. Abby is a fierce believer in the healing power of the arts. She has worked for the past 17 years teaching in public schools, enfusing the power of the creative into her classrooms. She is Amherst Writers and Artists certified and is the Co-Founder and Executive Director of Sidewalk Poets, a non profit organization that helps to amplify voices of underserved communities through writing and storytelling. Learn more about it at www.sidewalkpoets.org and visit her here: www.abbytempletongreene.com.

www.ingramcontent.com/pod-product-compliance
Lightning Source LLC
Chambersburg PA
CBHW030224170426
43194CB00007BA/857